DRAW
WITH A
VENGEANCE

DRAW WITH A VENGEANCE

Get Even in Ink
and Let Karma Handle the Rest

Helen Wrath

RUNNING PRESS
PHILADELPHIA · LONDON

© 2016 by Helen Wrath
Published by Running Press,
A Member of the Perseus Books Group

All rights reserved under the Pan-American and International Copyright Conventions

Printed in the United States

Books published by Running Press are available at special discounts for bulk purchases in the United States by corporations, institutions, and other organizations. For more information, please contact the Special Markets Department at the Perseus Books Group, 2300 Chestnut Street, Suite 200, Philadelphia, PA 19103, or call (800) 810-4145, ext. 5000, or e-mail special.markets@perseusbooks.com.

ISBN 978-0-7624-5919-3
Library of Congress Control Number: 2015934577

9 8 7 6 5 4 3 2 1
Digit on the right indicates the number of this printing

Cover design by Joshua McDonnell
Interior design by Bill Jones
Edited by Jordana Tusman
Typography: Conduit, Contempoprary Brush, and Huggable

Running Press Book Publishers
2300 Chestnut Street
Philadelphia, PA 19103-4371

Visit us on the web!
www.runningpress.com

Introduction

We all know someone who'd make even Mother Teresa reach for brass knuckles. Perhaps for you it's an unfaithful partner, an unreasonable boss, or a relative who should focus on her own train-wreck-of-a-life instead of commenting on yours! Let's call this person X, because "asinine, egotistical imbecile" takes up too much space. If you've ever imagined serving up sweet justice on X in ways that would probably require a large legal defense fund, turn to this book instead. On the following pages you'll find dozens of suggestions for doodles so you can inflict well-deserved retribution at X on paper. You don't have to do bad things to bad people. Get even in ink—and let karma handle the rest. And after you've drawn your revenge and enjoyed a cathartic round of primal screaming, go ahead and treat yourself to something nice. You deserve it.

Draw X's tiny, tiny brain
(and other
disproportionately small
body parts)
under the slide.

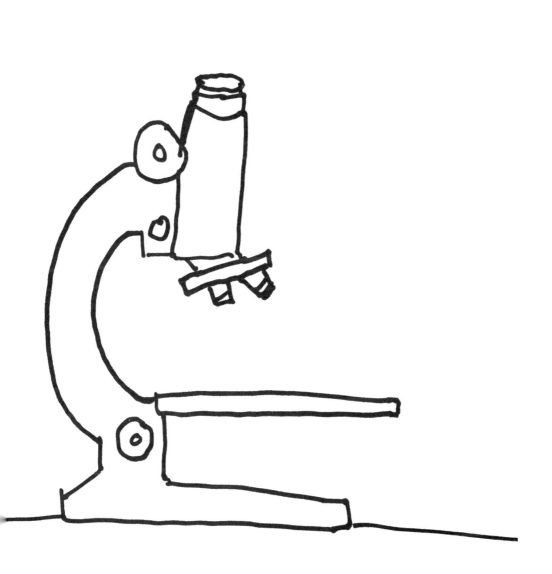

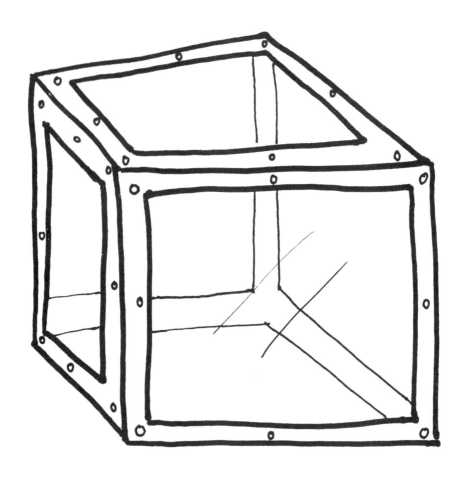

Draw X in the box. Draw locks and chains on the box.
Do not draw air holes.

Draw X here. Tear this page out and pour boiling coffee on it.
Do not caution X that the contents may be HOT!

X

FEEL THE BURN

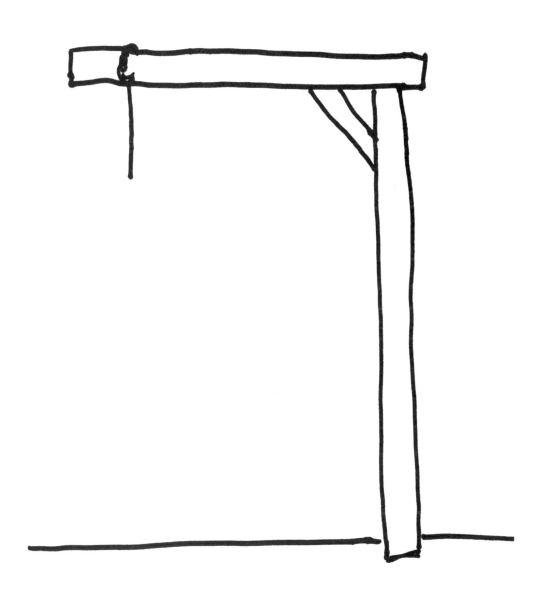

Draw small lines for each letter in X's name. Guess the wrong letters on purpose and hang X as you go.

Draw X here, wrapped up nice and tight.
Draw more menacing spiders.

Draw X here. Put on heavy boots.
Tear this page out and stomp on X.

X

HASTA LA VISTA

Draw X with an open wound.

Draw X in the hourglass. Draw lots and lots of sand.
Fill the hourglass.

Cut out letters from a magazine. Turn them into words
that describe exactly how you feel about X
and glue them to the page.

Draw X beneath
the boulder.
Draw yourself on top
of the boulder, seated
comfortably.

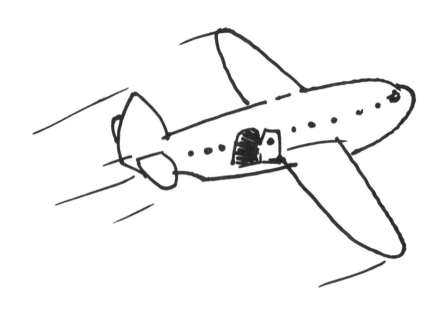

Draw X skydiving.
Forget to draw X's parachute.

Draw X here. Tear out this page and use it to clean anything gross on your bathroom floor.

X

SCRUB-A-DUB-DUB

Draw X here. Tear this page out and take it to the gym.
Tape X to the punching bag. Exercise your fists.

TAKE THAT

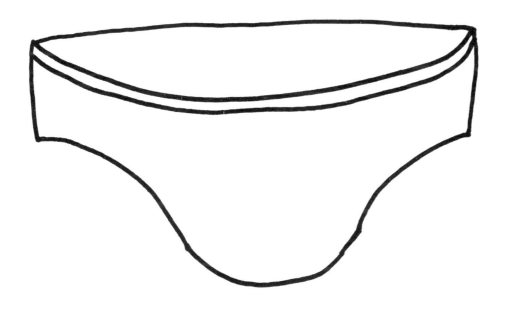

Draw X's underwear.
Put whatever you want in them.
Might we suggest pepper spray?

Draw a plank.
Then draw X on the plank.
Now erase the plank.

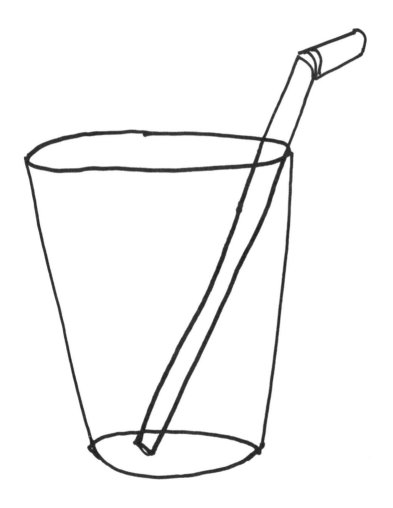

Draw X sipping from the straw.
Draw what X is sipping.

Draw X's face. Cover X's mouth with duct tape.
Lots and lots of duct tape.

DID YOU SAY
SOMETHING?

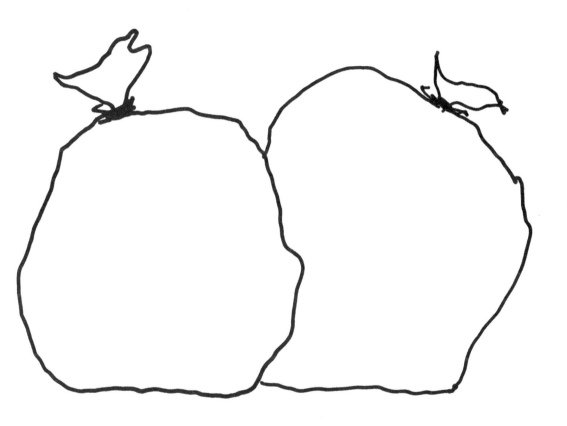

In the trash bags, write down the dumbest things X has ever said to you. Now tear this page out and toss it in the garbage!

X

PEE-YEW

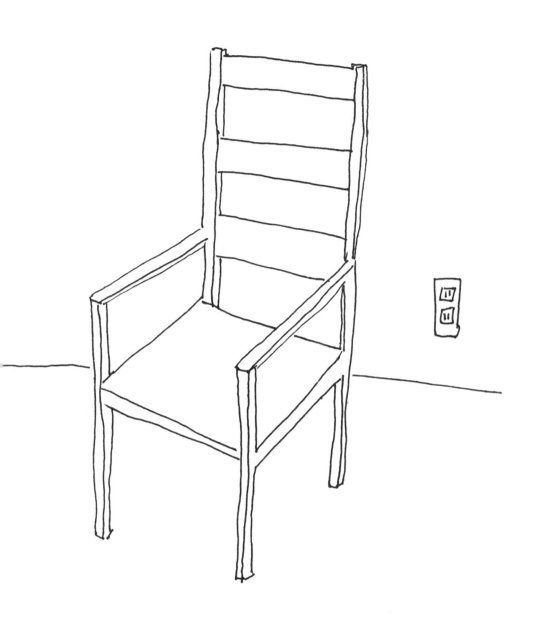

Draw X in the chair. Add wrist and ankle straps and maybe a metal headband. Now draw an electrical cord running from the chair to a big plug.
Make sure to draw the plug in the socket.

Draw something inside the cake, like razor blades or a live opossum. Tear the page out and give it to X on X's birthday.

HAPPY
BIRTHDAY

Draw X here. Tear this page out. Trample it.
Crumple it. Kick it. Throw it at the wall. Shred it.
Drink water afterward to rehydrate.

X

I GET SUCH A KICK
OUT OF YOU

Draw X with antlers and a fluffy white tail.

Draw X at the bottom
of the mountain.
Now draw an avalanche
rolling down the mountain
toward X.

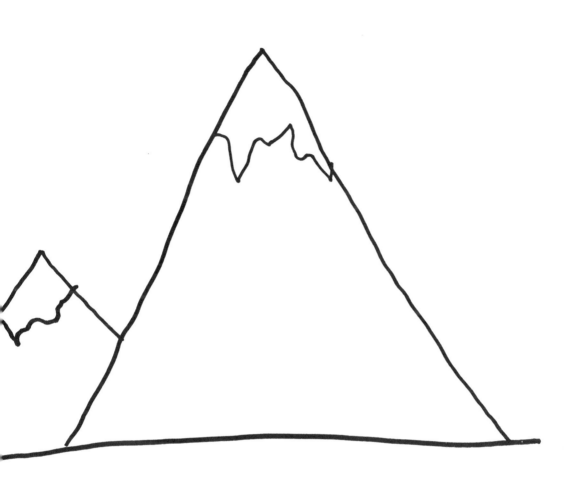

Design a flashy billboard
to tell the world
just how horrible X is.

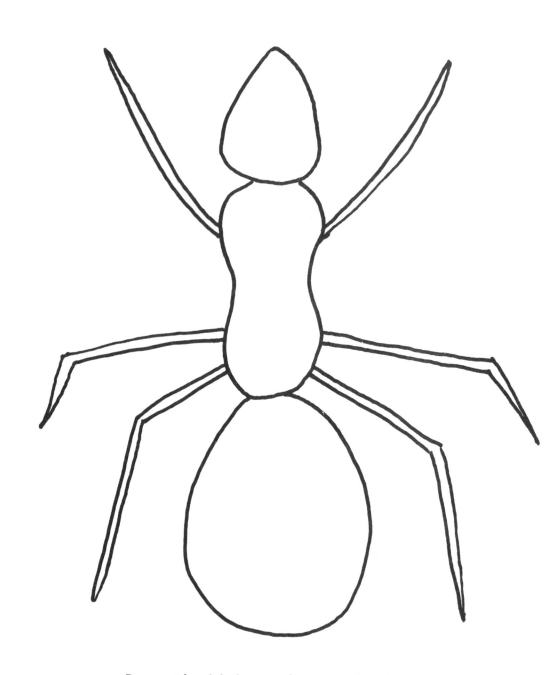

Draw X with bug wings and antennae.
Smack X with a flyswatter.

Draw X with open arms.
Then tear out this page and use it to pick up dog poo.

YOU'VE FINALLY FOUND YOUR CALLING

Fill in the blank, tear out the certificate,
and go post it somewhere.

WORST OF THE WORST

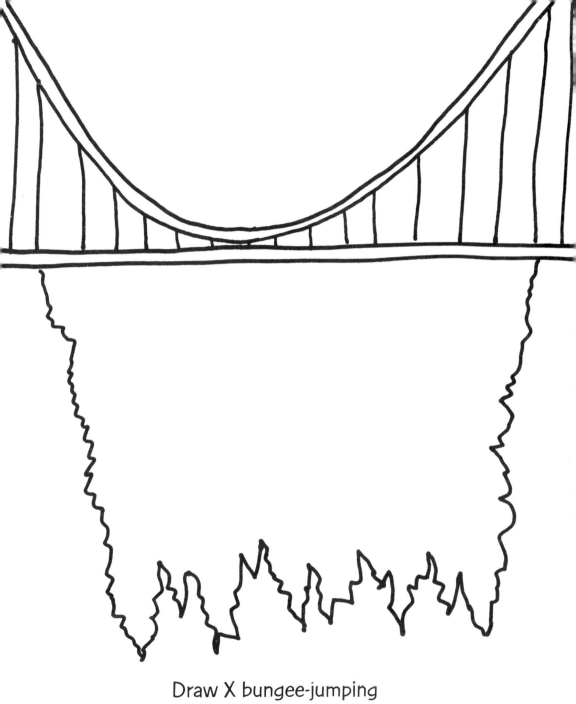

Draw X bungee-jumping
off this bridge. Get scissors and cut the cord.

Draw X in this pit.
Draw snakes.

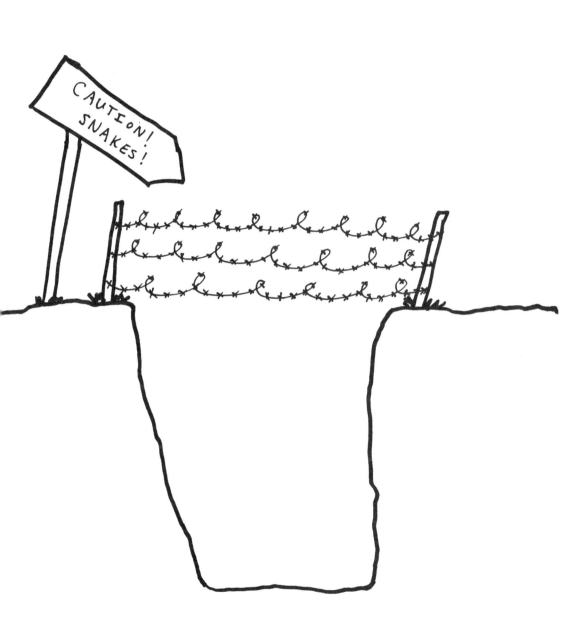

Draw X in a meat bikini.

Make a teeny, tiny doodle of X.
See if you can stab your pen exactly through X's center.

Draw X here. Catch a cold. Tear this page out.
Blow your nose on this page.

S'NOT FUNNY

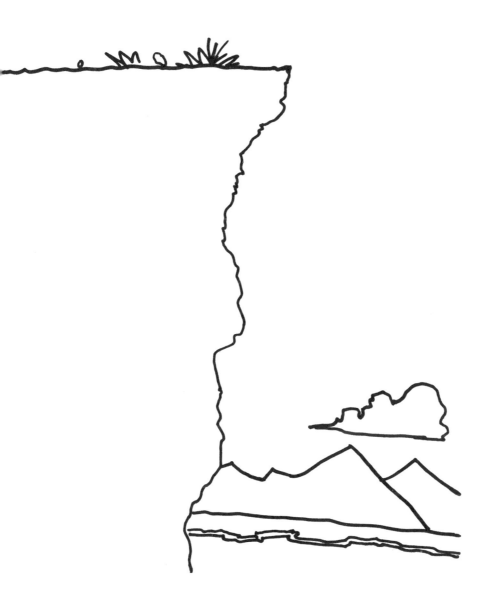

Draw X holding onto the edge of this cliff. Get a
hammer. How hard can you hit all ten of X's fingertips?

Draw X in the tub.
Draw a toaster falling
in the tub. Make sure the
toaster is plugged in.

Draw X on the weight bench. Draw a long bar across X's
chest. Draw weights on the ends of the bar.
Add lots and lots of weights.

Draw X here. Tear this page out and tape it
to a firecracker. Light the fuse.

HAVE A BLAST

Pick a diagnosis for X. Draw X experiencing
socially uncomfortable symptoms.

Draw X on the island.
Draw yourself on the luxury
ocean liner pulling away
from the island. Wave
goodbye with one finger.

Draw X just below the waves. Give X cement shoes.

Draw X here. Enjoy a large, fiber-rich meal. Tear this page out and drop it in the toilet. Then feel sweet relief.

X

FEELING FLUSHED?

Draw X floating in space wearing a spacesuit.
Now tear a hole in X's spacesuit.

Draw X here.
Color X a vivid red.

Draw X in the pot.
Draw a fire beneath the pot.
Draw the witches with
scowls on their faces
because X is too bitter.

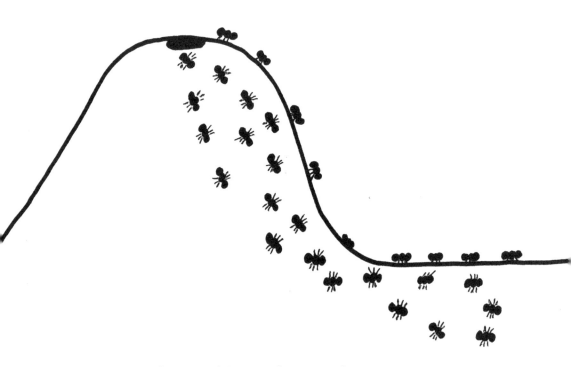

Draw X here. Smear X with honey.
Add more fire ants enjoying the honey.

Draw X here. Tear this page out and cut it into tiny
confetti pieces. Get yourself a glass of your favorite adult
beverage. Toss the confetti in the air. It's a party!

X

PULL YOURSELF TOGETHER

Draw X accidentally falling into this running wood chipper. Feel free to shred this page and use it for mulch.

Draw a voodoo doll of X.
Poke pins through X.

Draw X rolling nude in this poison ivy patch.

Draw X here. Tear this page out and crumple it into
a tiny ball. Get a golf club. Fore!

FEELING A BIT ROUGH?

Draw X here. X's flight has been delayed for several hours on the tarmac. Cough on X for added realism.

Draw X in a passionate embrace with this prickly cactus.

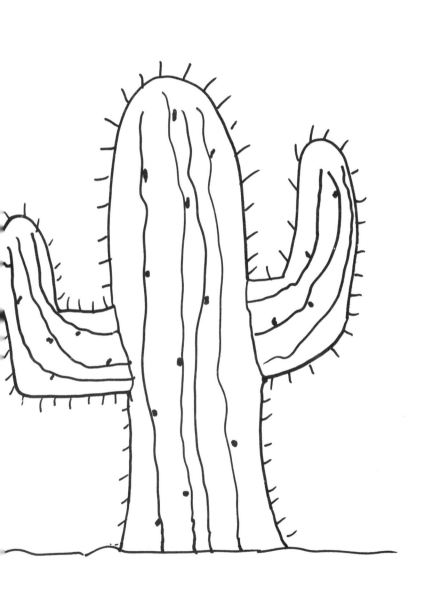

Draw X wearing this shirt.
Tear the page out and pin it
to a wall. Get darts.
How many times can you
hit the bullseye?

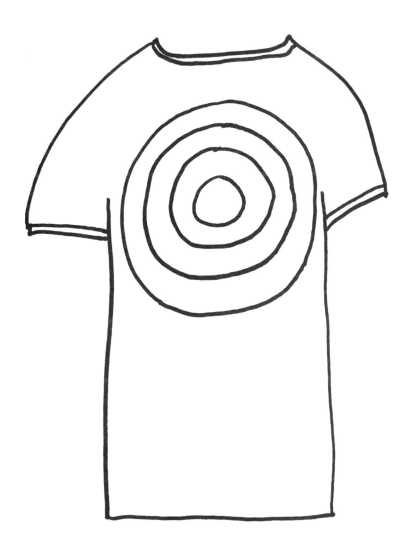

GET THE POINT?

Draw lots of hungry little lice on the comb.
Draw X using the comb.

Draw X here
hugging a tall,
wet, metal pole.

Draw X nude.

Draw X's face here. Give X piercings like upper and lower lip rings with a short chain firmly linking them.

Draw X wearing this chastity belt. Don't bother drawing a key.

Draw the hot sun shining on this bowl of rancid tuna salad. Draw X eating the entire bowl of tuna salad.

Draw X popping
out of the center hole.
Get a mallet. Win.
Keep winning.

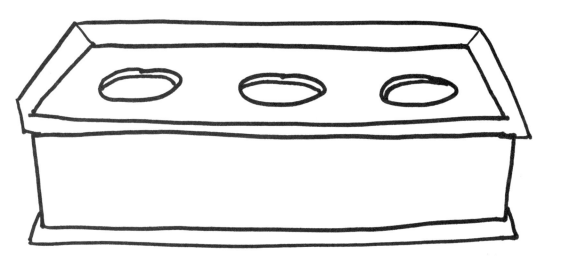

Draw X stuck in this maze. Seal off all exits.

Draw X with 100 tiny cuts. Tear this page out.
Squeeze fresh lemon juice all over X.

WHEN LIFE GIVES YOU LEMONS, USE THEM

Draw X trapped in a room
with all the other whiny babies.

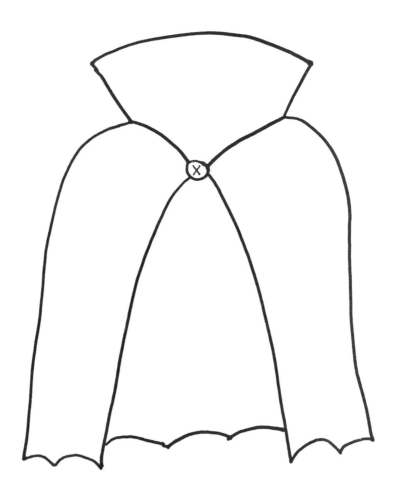

Draw X as a vampire. Give X fangs.
Pretend your pencil is a stake.

Write every horrible thing you've ever wanted to say to X. Tear this page out and burn it so it can't be used in a court of law.

GUILTY AS CHARGED

Draw X's face. Write your favorite descriptive word on X's forehead in permanent marker.

Draw X wearing a "Motorcycles are for Sissies" T-shirt.

Draw X here. Tear this page out and fold it into a paper airplane. Light a roaring fire. Make X crash and burn.

CRASH AND BURN

Draw X impaled upon the unicorn's horn.

Draw an open-mouthed X in the chair. Then draw a blindfold on the dentist. Now draw the inevitable outcome.

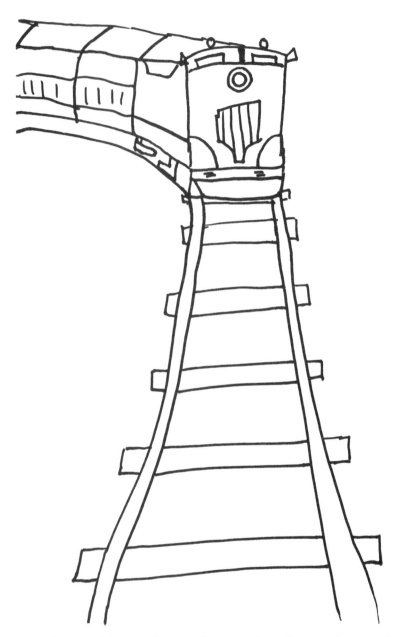

Draw X on the train tracks. Draw lots of rope tied in strong knots to keep X securely in place.

Draw X here. Tear this page out and take it to the top of the tallest building you can find. Throw X over the edge.

DON'T LOOK DOWN

Draw X in a banana suit.

Draw X getting probed.

Draw X here. Tear this page out and tape it to a piñata.
Get a bat. Skip the blindfold.

X

I'LL TAKE A WHACK AT THAT

Draw X here. Tear this page out and pin it to the bulletin board at the post office.

MISSING PERSON
NOT MISSED

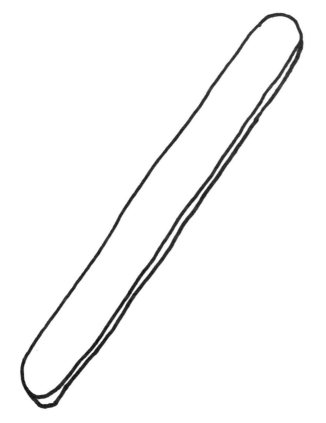

Draw X impaled upon this popsicle stick. Tear out this page and stick in the freezer so X can chill out for once.

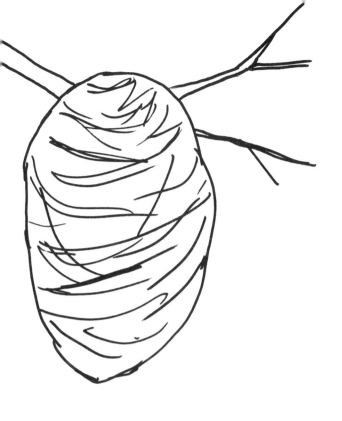

Draw a blindfolded X
smacking the wasps' nest like it's a piñata.

Draw X on this slab of meat.
Get a meat tenderizer.
Tenderize X.

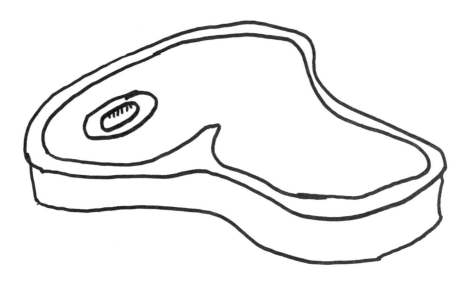

Feel better now?
Share your best
payback-via-pen
on Twitter
and Instagram:
#DWAV